TACOS

TACOS

AUTHENTIC MEXICAN TACOS
THE PLAYA TAKERIA WAY

RICARDO AMARE DEL CASTILLO

To my father and mother, Jorge and Deyanira,
for helping me to follow my dreams.

CONTENTS

INTRODUCTION	9
THE PERFECT TACO	15
BEEF TACOS	20
LAMB TACOS	40
PORK TACOS	56
CHICKEN TACOS	74
SEAFOOD TACOS	96
VEGETARIAN TACOS	112
BASICS & SAUCES	130
INDEX	154

INTRODUCTION

This is a book of favorite taco recipes from Ricardo Amare del Castillo, a passionate Mexican boy who left home in his 20s and went on to become a restauranteur and a representative of modern Mexico half way around the world in Australia.

Coming from one of the oldest civilizations on the planet, Ricardo has followed his passion to establish restaurants that recreate authentic Mexican experiences. He has helped develop various Mexican restaurants but still wants to fulfill his dream of opening taquerias and restaurants across the different countries, to make the Taco famous around the world. This is Ricardo's journey.

・・・・・・

I'll never forget my first smell of tacos as a child and the barbacoa tacos that we used to share with the family on Sundays. We Mexicans say that the way a taco makes you feel is hard to describe. For me and for many Mexicans, 'Tacos are life, and life is tacos'.

I started my career in International Business and Entrepeneurship which I stdied in México at Universidad Anahuac. After that, I decided to venture into some exciting projects, all focused on representing Mexico in a modern, contemporary way.

As a passionate foodie, I explored the culinary culture of my adopted country and saw a gap in the market – I had not discovered any truly authentic Mexican restaurants that gave customers the full Mexican experience. So after months of planning and finding investors, I opened a restaurant called Señoritas. I flew in a Mexican chef, brought in Mexican artifacts and pottery from different regions of Mexico and the restaurant took off.

Señoritas was a great success during the first year and I am sure its authenticity was the reason. As success followed success, the investors wanted to make changes and the authentic experience (in my opinion) was lost so it was time for me to move on, to leave my first baby and to find something new.

INTRODUCTION

I still believed that I could create a 'real Mexico' in this country. I kept searching for the right place to showcase great Mexican food. So I developed a new concept of taquerias with a friend of mine Vince. The restaurant was to be called Si Señor Art Taqueria, inspired by a neighborhood of Mexico City called Condesa. The result was a taco restaurant to show customers the real taste of tacos as they are served in Mexico. It became the place where friends and lovers of Mexican food would gather to share. Si Señor became the success it was with the help of a chef who came from Guadalajara in Mexico.

Six months after the opening, I was ready for new challenges. I wanted to find a place that resembled one of the Mexican Caribbean regions, Playa del Carmen. I had lived there for six months as a teenager and had wonderful memories especially of the intense blue color of the Mexican Caribbean. So I moved to Sydney.

My first job was to visit all the restaurants with Mexican food, and to check out restaurants that were considered to be the very best at the time. I loved to hear the way the owners of restaurants talk about Mexican food. Yet I felt that something was missing. After my research, I knew I was on the right track to start a Mexican restaurant in my new city replicating the unique atmosphere on a Mexican restaurant.

Eventually I opened my restaurant, Playa Takeria, in honor of Playa del Carmen in Mexico; a small taqueria in a swish inner-city area. Playa encapsulates many things: the Mexican art on the walls, the music, the authentic food, the staff, the chefs. I was able to find a Mexican chef from Playa del Carmen, Alejandro Urbina, who loves tacos as much as I do and seems to encapsulate the very essence of Mexican cooking.

Chef Alejandro Urbina, one of the best Mexican chefs in the country, has a way of preparing Mexican food that is simply sublime. He understands and distinguishes the different seasons of many Mexican regions, all of which are unmistakable in his food.

Since those first days and nights, Alejandro decided to follow his personal dreams and I was fortunate to find Mexican chef Diego Sotelo, who had travelled throughout Mexico experimenting with different flavors.

During the writing of this book, Playa Takeria was named one of the best Mexican restaurants in Sydney and some of the best representative of Mexican Taquerias in Australia.

INTRODUCTION

The intention of Playa was not only to create a restaurant but a window to Mexico, a place where families and friends can come and experience tacos, cervezas and tequilas.

There are thousands of possible combinations for tacos, but in this book we have selected what we think are the best ways to make, prepare and serve tacos so that you can offer your family or friends an authentic Mexican experience.

In Mexico the best time to taste a good taco is, well, anytime—from the morning, all through the day, at dinner and late into the night.

The origin of the tacos goes back to the Aztec culture, since the main ingredient of them is the corn, simple but without doubt a great food. Then the tacos are adorned with sauces that fuse together to create great tastes and give color to the dishes.

Of course everyone in Mexico has their opinion about what makes a taco great: from the south to the north of Mexico—from Tijuana to Playa del Carmen. What is true is that there are many varieties of tacos—meat, fish, bean and vegetable.

This book allows home cooks and chefs to discover the wonder of many taco creations and to share with family and friends.

Please enjoy.

THE PERFECT TACO

TORTILLAS

From the Aztecs to the taquerias of today, corn tortillas have been the foundation of Mexican cuisine. A quality tortilla is essential to a quality taco experience. Like bread, tortillas are best made and served fresh. We produce our homemade, gluten- and preservative-free corn tortillas and totopos (cornchips) in our restaurant kitchen throughout the day.

Some of the best tacos are those you find in a Mexican market. In the market, you will see the tortilleras, ladies who sell tortillas, by the dozen. You can buy the tortillas of different colors, blue (made of blue corn), red ones that have some kind of chili in them, and other varieties that represent the creativity of the cooks. Without a doubt, the tortilla is the most important part of making a great taco.

SALSAS

Salsas are the cornerstones of Mexican kitchens and are an accompaniment to every meal and as varied as Mexico itself. We make our own salsas from fresh vegetables, chilies, spices and natural seasonings avoiding canned, bottled and pre-packaged ingredients containing preservatives or additives. All our salsas are available in our restaurants and are available for purchase.

LIMONES AND GARNISHES

In Mexico limes are used to add some citrus kick to our tacos. Some of the best Taquerias across Mexico provide customers with an array of garnishes such as: coriander, potato, cactus, a variety of chillis, guacamole, onion, refried beans and cheeses. With such a range, everyone can make their taco unique.

INGREDIENTS AND SUBSTITUTES

Chambray onions (pearl onions) are very small onions valued for their sweet, delicate flavor. They can be creamed, roasted, or glazed. If unavailable, French shallots or small brown onions can be substituted.

Guajillo chilies are a variety of mild to medium hot peppers that are used extensively in Mexican cooking. They are often used in recipes with ancho and/or chipotle chillies.

Serrano chilies are a smaller version of the Jalapeño chili. They give a spicy kick to any recipe. If you can't find them, use Jalapeños instead.

Blue corn (also called Hopi maize) is grown in Mexico and some southern US states. With a sweet taste, the corn is ground to make corn meal to make the tortillas. This type of corn will make your tortillas Blue. This is the same process used to create Corn Tortillas.

Morita chilies are often purchased dried. To rehydrate, place in a bowl with enough water to cover and microwave for 60–90 seconds. The flavor is sweet with the subtle taste of smoky chocolate, licorice, cherries and coffee. They may be difficult to find in grocery stores. A good substitute is the chipotle chili.

Mulato chilies are mild to medium dried chilies that are most often used in Mexican mole sauces. Ranked very low on the heat scale, they have a soft smoky flavor with a taste similar to chocolate and licorice. Substitute with ancho chiles or if you can't source these either, cayenne pepper. Chilles are a crucial part on authentic Mexican recipes. Mexico has hundreds of chilli varities which are hard to find in the rest of the world. However, due to how popular Mexican Cuisine is there are distributors found in most places.

Piloncillo, very widely used in Mexico, is unrefined sugar made from cane sugar that is boiled and evaporated then pressed into blocks, rounds or cones. It is also known as panocha or panela in other countries. If you cannot find piloncillo, use brown sugar as a substitute.

Julienne is a method of cutting food into matchstick-sized pieces about ⅓ cm (⅑ in) thick and 7½ cm (3 in) long.

Carnitas, originating from the province of Michoacán in Mexico, literally means 'little meats'. Carnitas Tacos are made by braising or simmering the pork in lard until tender.

Manchego cheese originates from Le Mancha in Spain and is made traditionally from unpasteurized goat's milk. If you cannot find this cheese, substitute with Pecorino Romano or even cheddar, Gruyère or a Monterey Jack.

Achiote is used extensively in Mexican cooking to add color and flavor. Made from annatto seeds, it is sometimes called the 'saffron of Mexico'. The flavor is described as being a very mild nutty, musky and earthy. It may be difficult to get (try online). If you can't source it, a good substitute is turmeric or paprika or a mixture of both.

Poblano chilies are mild to medium in heat. One of the most commonly used chilies in Central Mexican cooking, they are used fresh and dried (dried poblanos are also called ancho chilies. If you can't find them, substitute with a mild chili such as jalapeño.

Salpicon in Spanish means 'medley' or 'hodgepodge'. In Mexican cooking, it refers to a salad mix that includes chili, tomato and avocado.

Serrano peppers get their name from the area of Mexico where they originated, the states of Puebla and Hidalgo. They are hotter than the more well known Jalapeno pepper which is the best substitute if you cannot source serrano peppers.

Epazote (pronounced eh-pah-ZOH-teh) is a herb used in the cuisines of central and southern Mexico and Guatemala. It has a pungent flavor with hints of oregano, anise, citrus, mint, and even tar. If you can't source it fresh, dried epazote can be found at specialty herb shops or online.

Panela cheese (queso panela) is a white, smooth cheese from Mexico made of pasteurized cow's milk. If unavailable, substitute with ricotta.

Oaxaca cheese is a style of Mexican cheese, which is a great flavor boost. If you can't find some then a similar cheese that could be used is Buffallo Mozzarella.

Pico de gallo literally means 'beak of rooster'. It is also called salsa fresca.

BEEF TACOS

TROPICAL TACOS

SERVES 4

- 40 ml (1⅓ fl oz) vegetable oil
- 150 g (5 oz) onion, chopped
- 1 garlic clove, finely chopped
- 500 g (17½ oz) fillet steaks, cut into squares
- 100 g (3½ oz) fresh pineapple, cubed
- 125 g (4 oz) mango, diced
- salt and pepper, to taste
- 4 large corn tortillas
- Guacamole (see sauces)

Heat a frypan on the stovetop. Add the oil then the onion and garlic and sauté for 2 minutes.

Add the beef strips to brown and season to taste.

When the meat is brown but still tender, add the pineapple and mango cubes and cook for a further 3 minutes.

Heat tortillas in the oven for 1–2 minutes. Alternatively, heat a frypan and add the tortillas, one at a time. Cook for 1–2 minutes each side. Keep warm while you heat the rest of the tortillas.

Place tortillas on plates. Add filling to each and top with guacamole to serve.

BEEF TACOS

TACOS DE ALAMBRE

SERVES 4

- 400 g (14 oz) beef, cut into strips
- pinch of salt and pepper, to taste
- olive oil, for frying
- ½ red capsicum (bell pepper), cut into strips
- ½ green capsicum (bell pepper), cut into strips
- 4 chambray onions, finely sliced
- 1 garlic clove, chopped
- 100 g (3½ oz) bacon strips, sliced and cubed
- 100 g (3½ oz) ham, diced
- 30 ml (1 fl oz) Worcestershire sauce
- 100 g (3½ oz) tasty cheddar cheese, cubed
- 4 large corn tortillas

Heat a frypan on the stove top until hot. Season the beef, add to the pan to brown. Turn and brown on the other side. The beef should be well browned on the outside and tender on the inside. Remove and set aside to rest.

Pour the oil into the pan to coat the bottom. Add the peppers and sauté until soft. Add the onion, garlic, bacon and ham. Cook for about 4 minutes stirring continually.

Add reserved meat and Worcestershire sauce.

Reduce the liquid and add the cheese. Stir for 1 minute or until the cheese melts.

Heat tortillas in the oven for 1–2 minutes. Alternatively, heat a frypan and add the tortillas, one at a time. Cook for 1–2 minutes each side. Keep warm while you heat the rest of the tortillas.

Place tortillas on plates. Add filling to each and serve.

Note: Chambray onions (pearl onions) are very small onions valued for their sweet, delicate flavor. They can be creamed, roasted, or glazed. If these are unavailable, French shallots or small brown onions can be substituted.

BEEF TACOS

FAJITA TACOS

SERVES 4

- 1 chicken wing
- 300 ml (10 fl oz) water
- ½ garlic clove, finely chopped
- 2 tablespoons onion, finely chopped
- salt and pepper, to taste
- 2½ tablespoons vegetable oil
- 400 g (14 oz) beef rump steak
- 2 tablespoons vegetable oil, for frying
- 5 ripe tomatoes, seeded and diced
- 1 tablespoon onion, finely chopped
- 2 green chilies, finely chopped (seeded optional)
- salt, to taste
- 4 corn tortillas
- sour cream, optional
- Guacamole (see sauces), optional

Preheat oven to 180–190°C (350–375°F) for heating the tortillas (if using this method).

To make the chicken broth, wash and dry the chicken wing with a paper towel.

Add the chicken, water, onion, garlic and salt and pepper to a saucepan and bring to the boil. Cook for 5 minutes. Remove from heat and set aside.

When cool, strain all solids and reserve the liquid.

In a hot saucepan, add the oil and beef and cook until brown on the outside but still tender inside.

Add tomato, onion, chillis and 100 ml (3½ fl oz) of the chicken broth. Add salt to taste.

Cook for 12 minutes over medium heat. Remove from heat and allow to cool slightly.

Heat tortillas in the oven for 1–2 minutes. Alternatively, heat a frypan and add the tortillas, one at a time. Cook for 1–2 minutes each side. Keep warm while you heat the rest of the tortillas.

Fill the hot tortillas with the steak mixture and serve with sour cream and guacamole if desired.

TINGA BEEF TACOS

SERVES 4

- 800 g (1 lb 10 oz) skirt steak, cubed
- 1½ L (3 pt) water
- salt, to taste
- 1 tablespoon vegetable oil
- 1 white onion, roughly chopped
- 1 garlic clove, chopped
- 6 red tomatoes, chopped and seeds removed
- 150 ml (5 fl oz) sour tomatoes (see sauces), mashed
- 1 chipotle chili, sliced
- 4 corn tortillas

Preheat oven to 180–190°C (350–375°F) for heating the tortillas (if using this method).

Cook the meat in a deep saucepan with enough water to cover for 6 hours (or 30 minutes in a pressure cooker, if you have one). Allow to cool for 30 minutes.

In a very hot saucepan, add oil and sauté the onion and garlic.

Add the tomatoes, the sour tomatoes and chili. Season with salt and cook for 5 minutes.

Add the meat and cook for another 5 minutes. Remove from heat.

Heat tortillas in the oven for 1–2 minutes. Alternatively, heat a frypan and add the tortillas, one at a time. Cook for 1–2 minutes each side. Keep warm while you heat the rest of the tortillas.

Serve mixture over hot tortillas.

BEEF TACOS

ARRACHERA TACO

SERVES 4

- 500 g (17½ oz) beef flank steak
- 200 ml (6¾ fl oz) dark beer (dark lager, brown ale or stout)
- 1 tablespoon beef stock
- 1 tablespoon Worcestershire sauce
- 4 lemons, juiced
- 3 garlic cloves, minced
- salt, to taste
- 4 corn tortillas

Preheat oven to 180–190°C (350–375°F) for heating the tortillas (if using this method).

In a large bowl, add the meat. Pour over with beer, seasoning sauce, Worcestershire sauce, lemon juice and garlic. Season with salt. Cover the bowl and refrigerate for 1 hour.

On a hot barbecue plate or frypan, cook the meat for 3–5 minutes on each side or until cooked to your liking. Remove from the plate and cut the meat into strips.

Heat tortillas in the oven for 1–2 minutes. Alternatively, heat a frypan and add the tortillas, one at a time. Cook for 1–2 minutes each side. Keep warm while you heat the rest of the tortillas.

Serve the steak on hot tortillas.

BEEF TACOS

RIB EYE TACO WITH POTATOES AND PARSLEY

SERVES 4

- 800 g (1lb 10 oz) rib eye
- salt and pepper, to taste
- 1½ L (3 pt) water
- salt, to taste
- 2 large potatoes
- 70 g (2½ oz) butter
- 1 garlic clove, chopped
- 2½ tablespoons parsley, washed and chopped
- 4 wheat flour tortillas
- Guacamole (see sauces), to serve

Preheat oven to 180–190°C (350–375°F) for heating the tortillas (if using this method).

Season the meat with salt and pepper. On a hot barbecue (or in a frypan), cook the rib eye until medium rare, turning to brown each side. Rest for 1 minute then cut into cubes. Set aside.

Peel the potatoes and dice into small cubes.

Add the water to a pot with salt and potatoes. Bring to the boil then turn to simmer for 15 minutes (start timing as soon as the water is boiling). Drain and set aside.

In a hot frypan, melt the butter. Add potatoes, garlic and parsley and sauté for 5 minutes. Add rib eye cubes and cook for a further 3 minutes.

Heat tortillas in the oven for 1–2 minutes. Alternatively, heat a frypan and add the tortillas, one at a time. Cook for 1–2 minutes each side. Keep warm while you heat the rest of the tortillas.

Serve steak and potato mix hot on the tortillas with the guacamole.

BEEF TACOS

GUAJILLO BEEF TACOS

SERVES 4

- 800 g (1lb 10 oz) lean beef
- ½–1 tablespoon olive oil
- 4 flour tortillas

Marinade
- 1–2 teaspoons fine salt
- 1 teaspoon pepper
- 10 garlic cloves, minced
- 220 ml (7 fl oz) apple cider vinegar
- 220 ml (7 fl oz) olive oil
- 10 g (⅓ oz) guajillo chili, seeded and ground
- 3 g (⅛ oz) parsley, chopped
- 125 ml (4 fl oz) red wine
- 2 bay leaves
- 2 red capsicums (bell peppers), chopped

Place all the ingredients for the marinade in a bowl and stir thoroughly.

Cut the beef into pieces of 3 x 3 cm (1 x 1 in).

Add the cubed beef to the marinade, cover and allow to marinate in the refrigerator for at least five hours or overnight.

Remove the meat from the marinade reserving the liquid. Cook the beef in a covered saucepan for 2 hours (or pressure cooker for 1½ hours if you have one) or until the meat is tender.

Heat a frypan on the stovetop. Add the oil and meat with 150 ml (5 fl oz) of the marinade. Cook until the liquid reduces by half. Remove meat with a slotted ladle and place in a serving bowl.

Heat tortillas in the oven for 1–2 minutes. Alternatively, heat a frypan and add the tortillas, one at a time. Cook for 1–2 minutes each side. Keep warm while you heat the rest of the tortillas.

Serve beef hot on the tortillas.

Note: Guajillo chilies are a variety of mild to medium hot peppers that are used extensively in Mexican cooking. They are often used in recipes with ancho and/or chipotle chillies.

BEEF TACOS

GRILLED FILLET STEAK TACO

SERVES 4

- 1 teaspoon ground oregano
- 3 garlic cloves, chopped
- 3 bay leaves
- salt and pepper, to taste
- 50 ml (1¾ fl oz) olive oil
- 4 lemons, juiced
- 200 g (7 oz) rib steak
- 200 g (7 oz) Filete Mignon
- 200 g (7 oz) fillet steak
- 4 wheat flour tortillas
- Salsa Verde (see sauces), to serve

Preheat oven to 180–190°C (350–375°F) for heating the tortillas (if using this method).

In a bowl, add oregano, garlic, bay leaf, oil and lemon juice. Season with salt and pepper and stir to combine.

Spread the mixture over the meat covering all sides.

Heat a grill or barbecue plate to hot and grill the meat until brown, turn and grill the other side. Cook to your liking. Remove from heat and allow to cool slightly.

Cut the meat into strips.

Heat tortillas in the oven for 1–2 minutes. Alternatively, heat a frypan and add the tortillas, one at a time. Cook for 1–2 minutes each side. Keep warm while you heat the rest of the tortillas.

Serve the meat hot on warmed tortillas with the Salsa Verde.

BEEF TACOS

SIRLOIN ORANGE TACOS

SERVES 4

- ground pepper and salt, to taste
- 3 oranges, zest
- 2 spring onions (scallions), chopped
- 2 tablespoons olive oil
- 800 g (1lb 10oz) sirloin steak
- 4 corn tortillas

To serve
- ½ white onion, chopped
- 50 g (2 oz) coriander (cilantro), chopped
- add Salsa Verde or Salsa Roja (see sauces)

In a bowl mix together the pepper, salt, orange zest, spring onions and olive oil. Mix thoroughly and set aside for 30 minutes.

On a hot grill, roast the sirloin until it is cooked to your liking.

Cook the sirloin on a hot grill or in a frypan. Brown on both sides and cook to your preference but we recommend medium rare.

Remove the sirloin from the grill, pour over with orange zest mix and rest for 10 minutes

Cut the sirloin into thick strips and serve over hot tortillas with onions, coriander and your favorite sauce.

Heat tortillas in the oven for 1–2 minutes. Alternatively, heat a frypan and add the tortillas, one at a time. Cook for 1–2 minutes each side. Keep warm while you heat the rest of the tortillas.

Serve the steak on the tortillas with selected sauce/s.

BEEF TACOS WITH RED SAUCE

SERVES 4

- 500 g (17½ oz) beef steak, chopped
- 60 ml (2 fl oz) apple cider vinegar
- 2 garlic cloves, minced
- ½ teaspoon paprika
- ½ teaspoon oregano
- ½ teaspoon cumin
- salt and pepper, to taste
- 4 tortillas (or store-bought taco shells)
- red sauce (see sauces)
- 40 g (1½ oz) coriander (cilantro), roughly chopped
- 100 g (3½ oz) onion, finely chopped
- ½–1 tablespoon lemon juice

Add the steak, vinegar, garlic, paprika, oregano and cumin into a bowl. Mix together and season to taste. Cover and place in the refrigerator for 45 minutes. Remove and allow to come to room temperature.

Heat a frypan. Add oil and when hot, add the mixture and cook until the meat is browned but still tender inside.

Heat tortillas in the oven for 1–2 minutes. Alternatively, heat a frypan and add the tortillas, one at a time. Cook for 1–2 minutes each side. Keep warm while you heat the rest of the tortillas.

Divide into four portions and serve the beef mixture over hot tortillas. Add red sauce to taste. Sprinkle with chopped onion and cilantro leaves. Pour over with a little lemon juice and serve.

LAMB AND BEER TACOS

SERVES 4

- 150 ml (5 fl oz) vegetable oil
- 1 teaspoon salt
- 1 teaspoon pepper
- 1 kg (2.2 lb) lamb skirt, cut into cubes
- 3 pieces serrano chili, sliced
- 11 garlic cloves, finely chopped
- 800 ml (1½ pt) dark beer (dark lager, brown ale or stout)
- 1 teaspoon sugar
- 220 ml (7 fl oz) mashed tomato sour (see sauces)
- 4 corn tortillas

Note: Serrano chilies are a smaller version of the Jalapeño chili. They give a spicy kick to any recipe. If you can't find them, use Jalapeños instead.

Add the lamb, salt and pepper to a bowl and knead for 25 minutes with fingertips.

Heat a large frypan and add the vegetable oil until it is very hot. Add the lamb and brown on all sides.

Add the serrano chili, garlic and the beer. Cook for 8 minutes.

Add the sugar and the mashed tomato sour. Cook for a further 12 minutes without a cover and mix with the seasoning.

Heat tortillas in the oven for 1–2 minutes. Alternatively, heat a frypan and add the tortillas, one at a time. Cook for 1–2 minutes each side. Keep warm while you heat the rest of the tortillas.

Serve lamb on hot tortillas.

LAMB TACOS

LEG OF LAMB WITH APPLE TACOS

SERVES 4

- 70 ml (2½ fl oz) olive oil
- 900 g (2 lb) leg of boneless lamb, cut into cubes
- 1 teaspoon salt
- 3 garlic cloves, minced
- 50 g (1¾ oz) white onion, chopped
- 100 ml 3½ fl oz) white wine
- 150 ml (5 fl oz) honey
- 2 red apples, core removed and cut into segments
- 250 ml (8 fl oz) water
- 4 flour tortillas
- Salsa (see sauces), to serve

In a saucepan, heat the oil and sauté the meat with salt, garlic and onion.

When the meat begins to brown, add the white wine and scrape the bottom of the pan to get any baked on lamb.

Pour honey over the meat and cook for 3–4 minutes to caramelize.

Stir in the apples and pour in the water. Cover and cook for 20 minutes over medium heat.

Heat tortillas in the oven for 1–2 minutes. Alternatively, heat a frypan and add the tortillas, one at a time. Cook for 1–2 minutes each side. Keep warm while you heat the rest of the tortillas.

Serve on hot tortillas with the salsa.

LAMB TACOS

LAMB FILLET TACOS WITH SALSA MORITA

SERVES 4

- 650 g (23 oz) lamb fillet
- 1 teaspoon fine salt
- 1 teaspoon white pepper
- 30 g (1 oz) butter, softened
- 5 ml (1 teaspoon) lamb stock
- 5 ml (1 teaspoon) Worcestershire sauce
- ½ tablespoon vegetable oil

Morita sauce

- 2 tablespoons vegetable oil
- 2 garlic cloves
- 3 tablespoons onion, chopped
- 10 pieces dried morita chilis
- 4 tomatoes cut into 4 pieces
- water, as required
- salt, to taste
- chicken stock powder (or cubes), optional
- 4 flour tortillas
- 100 g (3½ oz) onion, finely chopped, to serve
- 100 g (3½ oz) coriander (cilantro), chopped, to serve

Season the lamb fillets with salt and pepper. Spread with the butter. Add seasoning juice and Worcestershire sauce.

Heat a frypan with a little oil. Add the lamb and fry on one side. Turn and fry on the other side. Cook to your liking. Remove from pan and set lamb aside.

To make the sauce, place the dried chilies in a microwave-safe bowl with enough water to cover. Microwave for 90 seconds then set aside.

Add the oil to a frypan. Add the garlic and onion and fry until translucent. Add the tomatoes and chilies and stir. Cook for a further 5 minutes. Add the water and boil until thick. Add the chicken stock powder to taste if you are using this. Add the meat and cook for 5 more minutes.

Heat tortillas in the oven for 1–2 minutes. Alternatively, heat a frypan and add the tortillas, one at a time. Cook for 1–2 minutes each side. Keep warm while you heat the rest of the tortillas.

Serve lamb fillets and morita sauce hot on tortillas. Sprinkle with chopped onion and cilantro to taste.

Note: Morita chilies are often purchased dried. To rehydrate, place in a bowl with enough water to cover and microwave for 60–90 seconds. The flavor is sweet with the subtle taste of smoky chocolate, licorice, cherries and coffee. They may be difficult to find in grocery stores. A good substitute is the chipotle chili.

MARINATED LAMB TACO

SERVES 4

- 800 g (1 lb 10 oz) lamb skirt (4 steaks)
- 4 flour tortillas
- Red sauce, to serve (see sauces)

Marinade
- 1 onion, cut into quarters
- 1 teaspoon salt
- ½ teaspoon black pepper
- ½ teaspoon nutmeg
- 2 bay leaves
- 2 sprigs thyme
- 10 g paprika powder
- 100 ml (3½ fl oz) red wine vinegar
- 2 garlic cloves, finely chopped

Preheat the oven to 200°C (400°F).

In a bowl mix together the ingredients of the marinade.

Add the meat to the marinade and mix thoroughly to coat. Allow to stand for 2 hours.

Place the steaks in a baking dish and spoon over with the marinade.

Cover steaks with foil and bake for about 20–25 minutes.

Remove from the oven and check that the meat is cooked. Cut each steak into two lengthwise.

Heat tortillas in the oven for 1–2 minutes. Alternatively, heat a frypan and add the tortillas, one at a time. Cook for 1–2 minutes each side. Keep warm while you heat the rest of the tortillas.

To serve, place two pieces of steak on each tortilla.

LEMON LAMB TACOS

SERVES 4

- 4 lamb shanks (approx. 250 g (8¾ oz) each)
- salt and pepper, to taste
- 4 corn tortillas

Marinade
- 2 lemons, zest and juice
- 130 ml (4½ fl oz) sherry
- 60 ml (2 fl oz) olive oil
- 2 garlic cloves, minced
- 2 tablespoons fresh parsley, chopped
- salt, to taste

In a large bowl, add the lemon juice and zest, sherry, olive oil, garlic, parsley and salt.

Season the lamb with salt and pepper.

Add the lamb shanks to the marinade and place in the refrigerator for 2 hours. Remove the shanks from the bowl.

Place the shanks on a baking dish and roast in the oven for 35–40 minutes, basting more marinade every 10 to 15 minutes. Turn them at about 20 minutes to brown on both sides

Remove from the oven and rest for 5–10 minutes.

Heat tortillas in the oven for 1–2 minutes. Alternatively, heat a frypan and add the tortillas, one at a time. Cook for 1–2 minutes each side. Keep warm while you heat the rest of the tortillas.

To serve, cut into strips and serve on the tortillas.

LAMB TACOS WITH COCONUT

SERVES 4

- 1.2 kg (2.6 lb) boneless lamb, cut into pieces
- 125 g (4½ oz) yellow capsicum (bell pepper), cut into cubes
- 350 ml (12 ⅓ fl oz) coconut water
- 150 g (5 oz) grated coconut
- 50 g (1¾ oz) chives, chopped
- 4 blue corn tortillas

Marinade

- 2 teaspoons salt
- 1 teaspoon ground black pepper
- 400 ml (13 fl oz) vegetable oil
- 60 g (2 oz) butter, melted
- 1 garlic clove, finely chopped

Note: Blue corn (also called Hopi maize) is grown in Mexico and some southern US states. With a sweet taste, the corn is ground to make corn meal to make the tortillas.

In a large bowl, mix all of the marinade ingredients together.

Add the lamb and marinate for 1 hour.

Heat a saucepan then add the lamb and cook over medium heat until brown.

Add capsicum, coconut water and the grated coconut and cook covered on a rolling simmer for 25 minutes.

Once the lamb is well cooked and the liquid has reduced by 60 per cent, add the chives and turn off the heat.

Heat tortillas in the oven for 1–2 minutes. Alternatively, heat a frypan and add the tortillas, one at a time. Cook for 1–2 minutes each side. Keep warm while you heat the rest of the tortillas.

Serve over hot tortillas.

LAMB TACOS

LAMB NECK TACOS WITH MOLE

SERVES 4

- 650 g (23 oz) lamb neck chops, cut into pieces
- 1 teaspoon fine salt
- 1 teaspoon ground black pepper
- 220 ml (7 fl oz) tequila
- 1 tablespoon olive oil
- 4 flour tortillas
- Mole sauce (see sauces)

Note: Chicken broth is made when making other recipes from this book. You may have kept the broth for other uses. Only use store purchased broth if you don't have your own.

Season the lamb pieces with salt and pepper and marinate them with tequila for 45 minutes.

Heat a frypan with the oil. Add the lamb pieces. Cook on one side for 3–5 minutes, they turn and cook the other side for 3–5 minutes. Remove from pan and rest for 5 minutes.

Heat tortillas in the oven for 1–2 minutes. Alternatively, heat a frypan and add the tortillas, one at a time. Cook for 1–2 minutes each side. Keep warm while you heat the rest of the tortillas.

Pour mole sauce over the lamb pieces. Serve with the hot tortillas.

You can serve all tacos on one big plate, allowing guest to serve themselves or, serve one per guest if a more intimate dinner.

LAMB TACOS

LAMB LOIN WITH PILONCILLO AND CHILI TACOS

SERVES 4

- 650 g (23 oz) lamb loin, chopped
- 1½ teaspoons fine salt
- 1 teaspoon ground black pepper
- 1 tablespoon vegetable oil
- 2 potatoes, washed, peeled and cut julienne
- vegetable oil
- salt, to taste
- 4 corn tortillas

Piloncillo sauce
- 1 tablespoon vegetable oil
- 1 garlic clove, finely chopped
- 4 serrano chilies, cut into 2½ cm (½ in) rings
- 220 ml (7 fl oz) soy sauce
- 440 ml (15 fl oz) orange juice
- 150 g (5 oz) grated piloncillo
- salt, to taste
- 20 g (3/4 oz) cornflour (corn starch)
- a little water

To make the sauce, heat a shallow frypan and add the oil. When medium hot, add the garlic and chilies. Stir and sauté for 2 minutes but do not brown. Add the soy sauce, orange juice and the piloncillo. Season with salt. Mix the cornflour with a little water to form a thick paste. Take the pan off the heat and mix in the corn starch. Put back on the hot plate and bring back to boil. The sauce needs to be thick, not runny.

Preheat oven to 200°C (400°F). Season the lamb with salt and pepper. Heat a frypan and add the oil. When hot, add the lamb and seal on all sides. Transfer lamb to a baking dish and add the sauce. Bake for 20 minutes then remove and allow to cool slightly. Cut the lamb into slices. Set aside.

To make the potato chips, dry the potatoes with paper towel or clean cloth. Heat oil in a deep frypan or saucepan. Test the temperature with one potato chip. If the oil sizzles immediately, add half the potatoes. Cook until chips are crisp on the outside. Remove with a slotted ladle and place on a wire rack to drain then repeat with the rest of the potatoes. Sprinkle with salt.

Heat tortillas in the oven for 1–2 minutes. Alternatively, heat a frypan and add the tortillas, one at a time. Cook for 1–2 minutes each side.

To serve, place the lamb slices on the tortillas with chips on the side.

PORK TACOS EN SALSA VERDE

SERVES 4

- 900 g (2 lb) pork shoulder
- 100 ml (3½ fl oz) vegetable oil
- 1 teaspoon pepper
- 2 garlic cloves, chopped
- 2 cloves
- 1 teaspoon cumin (optional)
- 4 corn tortillas

Green Salsa

- 800 ml (27 fl oz) water
- 250 g (8¾ oz) green jalapeno peppers
- 2 medium onions, quartered
- 1 red tomato
- 250 g (8¾ oz) green tomato (or tomatillo)
- 2 cloves
- 1 teaspoon cumin
- 1 teaspoon dried oregano
- 1 garlic clove, finely chopped
- salt, to taste

Pat dry the pork and cut into small squares.

Heat the oil in a wide-based pan over medium-high heat. Add the pork (in batches if necessary to avoid overcrowding). Add the pepper, clove, garlic and cumin if using. Brown the pork on all sides, about 8 minutes per batch. Set aside.

For the sauce, add water to a large saucepan. Add jalapeno peppers, onion, red and green tomatoes.

Bring to the boil and add cloves, cumin, oregano and garlic. Reduce to a simmer and cook for about 15 minutes.

Blend all cooked ingredients with little water into a blender.

Add the sauce to the frypan and cook with the pork for 15 minutes over a low heat.

Add salt to taste.

Heat tortillas in the oven for 1–2 minutes. Alternatively, heat a frypan and add the tortillas, one at a time. Cook for 1–2 minutes each side. Keep warm while you heat the rest of the tortillas.

Serve hot on tortillas

PORK TACOS

PORK CARNITAS – MICHOACAN STYLE

SERVES 4

- 700 g (1 lb 7 oz) lard
- 500 g (17½ oz) pork ribs
- 500 g (17½ oz) pork loin
- 500 g (17½ oz) pork belly
- 2 medium onions, peeled and cut in half lengthwise
- 1½ L (51 fl oz) water
- 125 ml (4 fl oz) milk
- 1 sweet orange, juice and peel
- aromatic herbs (1 teaspoon dried oregano, ¼ teaspoon ground cloves, 2 bay leaves, 1 teaspoon paprika)
- salt and pepper, to taste
- 4 corn tortillas
- guacamole (see sauces)

Heat the lard in a large frypan over high heat. Add the pork ribs, loin and belly (in batches if necessary) and brown on all sides. Add the onion and cook for a further 5 minutes until translucent.

Once the meat is browned, remove the onion.

Add the water, milk, orange juice and zest, and the herbs. Cook uncovered over medium heat for about 90 minutes.

Drain the meat and season with salt and pepper.

Heat tortillas in the oven for 1–2 minutes. Alternatively, heat a frypan and add the tortillas, one at a time. Cook for 1–2 minutes each side. Keep warm while you heat the rest of the tortillas.

Serve hot on tortillas with guacamole.

Note: Carnitas, originating from the province of Michoacán in Mexico, literally means 'little meats'.

PORK TACOS

SMOKED PORK CHOP TACOS

SERVES 4

- water
- 1 teaspoon fine salt
- 3 potatoes, washed and peeled
- 350 ml (12½ fl oz) vegetable oil
- 4 pieces smoked pork chop
- 30 ml (1 fl oz) olive oil
- 1 teaspoon ground black pepper
- 4 corn tortillas
- Mozarella cheese, to serve
- 60 g (2 oz) chilled onions (see sauces), to serve
- 4 tortillas

To cook the chops, add oil to a frypan or griddle. Sprinkle chops with pepper and fry in the hot pan, turning the chops to brown both sides. Remove and set aside.

Julienne the potatoes by cutting into matchstick-sized pieces about ⅓ cm (⅑ in) thick and 7½ cm (3 in) long. Dry the chips with paper towel or a clean cloth.

Heat oil in a deep frypan or saucepan. Test the temperature with one potato chip. If the oil sizzles immediately, add half the potatoes (to ensure the oil does not lose too much heat). Cook until chips are crisp on the outside. Remove with a slotted ladle and place on a wire rack to drain. Make sure the oil is hot again before cooking the rest of the potato chips. Remove and drain on a wire rack. Sprinkle with salt, to taste.

Heat tortillas in the oven for 1–2 minutes. Alternatively, heat a frypan and add the tortillas, one at a time. Cook for 1–2 minutes each side. Keep warm while you heat the rest of the tortillas.

Serve the cheeses on the tortillas some potato chips and chilled onion to finish.

PORK TACOS

POBLANA TINGA TACOS

SERVES 4

- 600 g (21 oz) pork mince
- 1 L (2 pt) water
- pinch of salt
- 45 ml (1½ fl oz) vegetable oil
- 1 garlic clove, chopped
- 1 onion, sliced
- 3 tomatoes, roasted
- 3 chipotle peppers
- ½ teaspoon sugar
- salt, to taste
- 4 wheat flour tortillas

To cook the pork mince, add to a pot and cover with water. Add a pinch of salt, bring to the boil and reduce heat. Simmer for 1 hour.

Remove meat from the broth (and reserve broth for freezing if you wish). Place the pork in a covered bowl and chill in the refrigerator.

To preparing the tinga, heat the oil in a frypan. Add the onion and garlic and sauté until translucent.

Add the garlic, onion tomatoes and peppers into a blender and pulse to make a smooth sauce.

Remove pork from the refrigerator. Add to a frypan with the tinga sauce. Season with salt to taste and cook for a further 5 minutes.

Heat tortillas in the oven for 1–2 minutes. Alternatively, heat a frypan and add the tortillas, one at a time. Cook for 1–2 minutes each side. Keep warm while you heat the rest of the tortillas.

Serve the pork in tinga sauce on the hot tortillas and add any salsa, we suggest red salsa.

PORK TACOS

PORK AND PEANUT TACOS

SERVES 4

- 600 g (21 oz) pork mince
- 1 L (34 fl oz) water
- pinch of salt
- 4 garlic cloves, chopped
- 50 g (1¾ oz) onion, chopped
- 165 g (5½ oz) peanuts, shelled and toasted
- 320 g (11¼ oz) roasted tomatoes (see sauces)
- 15 g (½ oz) sesame seeds
- salt and pepper, to taste
- 4 corn tortillas

To cook the pork, add to a large pot and cover with the water ¾ of the pot.

Add a pinch of salt, garlic and onion. Bring to the boil and reduce heat. Simmer for 1 hour.

Strain the pork and place in a bowl reserving the broth.

To make the peanut sauce place peanuts, tomatoes, sesame seeds, salt and pepper into a blender and grind to a paste. You may need to scrape the sides with a plastic spatula once or twice so that all the ingredients are combined well.

Add the sauce and the pork to a frypan and cook for 15 minutes.

Heat tortillas in the oven for 1–2 minutes. Alternatively, heat a frypan and add the tortillas, one at a time. Cook for 1–2 minutes each side. Keep warm while you heat the rest of the tortillas.

Serve the pork with peanut sauce on the hot corn tortillas.

PORK TACOS

PORK RIB TACOS WITH CHEESE

SERVES 4

- 1 white onion, chopped
- 2–3 tablespoons water
- 1 tablespoon sugar
- 120 g (4 oz) potatoes
- 600 g (21 oz) boneless pork rib
- salt and pepper, to taste
- 4 flour tortillas
- 120 g (4 oz) manchego cheese, cut into thin slices
- 1 onion, julienne
- 100 g (3½ oz) avocado, cut into wedges

Note: Manchego cheese originates from Le Mancha in Spain and is made traditionally from unpasteurized goat's milk. If you cannot find this cheese, substitute with Pecorino Romano or even cheddar, Gruyère or a Monterey Jack.

To make the caramelized onion, add the onions, water and sugar to a frypan, bring to boil and cook for 5–10 minutes or until the onions have caramelized. Set aside.

To cook the pork, season with salt and pepper. Heat a grill or barbecue to hot and add the pork. Grill until browned on all sides and cooked to your preference. Remove and allow to rest for 10 minutes then dice into pieces.

Julienne the potatoes by cutting into matchstick-sized pieces about ½ cm (⅙ in) thick and 7½ cm (3 in) long. Dry the chips in paper towel or a clean teatowel.

Heat oil in a deep frypan or saucepan. Test the temperature with one potato chip. If the oil sizzles immediately, add half the potatoes (to ensure the oil does not lose too much heat). Cook until chips are crisp on the outside. Remove with a slotted ladle and place on a wire rack to drain. Make sure the oil is hot again before cooking the rest of the potato chips. Remove and drain on a wire rack. Sprinkle with salt, to taste.

Heat tortillas in the oven for 1–2 minutes. Alternatively, heat a frypan and add the tortillas, one at a time. Cook for 1–2 minutes each side. Keep warm while you heat the rest of the tortillas.

To serve, place the cheese on the hot tortillas. Add the meat. Accompany with onions, fries and avocado wedges.

PORK TACOS

PORK APPLE TENDERLOIN TACOS

SERVES 4

- 900 g (2 lb) pork tenderloin, cut into large pieces
- 1–2 teaspoons salt
- 1–2 teaspoons pepper
- 60 ml (2 fl oz) oil
- 300 ml (10 fl oz) sour cream
- 1 teaspoon cornflour (corn starch)
- 50 g (1¾ oz) butter
- 3 red apples, cut into wedges
- 1 teaspoon sugar
- 2 lemons, juiced
- salt and pepper, to taste
- 4 flour tortillas
- 150 g (5 oz) guacamole (see sauces), to serve

Pat dry the pork and rub in the salt and pepper. Add the oil to a hot frypan. Add the pork and brown on all sides, about 5 minutes. Reduce the heat and cook for another 10 minutes.

Mix the sour cream and cornflour in a bowl. Add to the frypan and bring back to a boil. Turn off the heat and set aside.

Heat a frypan and melt the butter. Add the apples, sugar and lemon juice. Season to taste and cook 4 minutes.

Heat tortillas in the oven for 1–2 minutes. Alternatively, heat a frypan and add the tortillas, one at a time. Cook for 1–2 minutes each side. Keep warm while you heat the rest of the tortillas.

Serve the pork on the hot tortillas accompanied by apple sauce and guacamole.

PORK TACOS

TACOS AL PASTOR

SERVES 4

Pastor sauce

- 1 tomato
- 3 guajillo chilies, deseeded
- 2 Chiles de Arbol deseeded
- 2 chipotle peppers
- 2 garlic cloves, chopped
- 1 onion, roughly diced
- 50 ml (1¾ fl oz) white vinegar
- 110 ml (3¾ fl oz) orange juice
- 200 g (7 oz) pineapple, roughly cut
- 3 cloves
- ½ teaspoon ground cumin
- ½ teaspoon ground oregano
- 1 teaspoon salt
- 800 g (1 lb 10 oz) pork loin, cut into thin fillets
- 4 flour tortillas
- 80 g (2¾ oz) coriander (cilantro), roughly chopped
- 1 white onion, julienne
- 80 g (2¾ oz) pineapple

To make the pastor sauce, blister the tomato skin over a flame until it has burned and begins to peel, about 10 minutes. Peel, cut in half and discard seeds.

Add the guajillo and Chiles de Arbol chilies to a saucepan with 2 cups of water and boil until softened, about 5 minutes. Add chipotle peppers, garlic, onion, vinegar, orange juice, pineapple, cloves, cumin, oregano, the roasted tomatoes and Chiles de Arbol. In a blender, purée to a smooth sauce and chill for 15 minutes.

To prepare the meat, place in a bowl and cover with the sauce. Marinate in refrigerator for 4 hours.

Heat a frypan on the stovetop, add the meat and cook by turning it continuously and until it is cooked through and lightly browned.

Heat tortillas in the oven for 1–2 minutes. Alternatively, heat a frypan and add the tortillas, one at a time. Cook for 1–2 minutes each side. Keep warm while you heat the rest of the tortillas.

Cut the pineapple for serving into bite-sized pieces. Serve the pork over tortillas and sprinkle with coriander, onion and pineapple.

Note: Pastor in Mexican means shepherd. So Tacos al Pastor literally translates to 'tacos in the style of the shepherd. Traditionally this dish is made by spit-grilling the meat and pineapple. However, it can be cooked in a frypan to create authentic-tasting tacos al pastor. Originating in central Mexico, Lebanese immigrants brought their method of cooking meat with them – the shawarma spit-grilling process.

PORK TACOS

COCHINITA PIBIL TACOS

SERVES 4

- 30 g (1 oz) achiote paste
- 250 ml (8 fl oz) apple cider vinegar
- 1 teaspoon salt
- ½ teaspoon black pepper
- ½ teaspoon ground cumin
- ½ teaspoon ground oregano
- 1 onion, chopped
- 950 ml (32 fl oz) orange juice
- 800 g (1 lb 10 oz) leg of pork, cut in 2½ cm (1 in) pieces
- 1 banana leaf (optional)
- 1 teaspoon butter
- 4 large corn tortillas
- Salsa Habanero or Salsa Chipotle a mild option (see sauces)

Preheat the oven to 200° C (400°F).

Grind in the blender achiote, vinegar, salt, pepper, cumin, oregano, onion and orange juice.

Place the pork into a bowl and add the marinade. Blend well and set aside to marinate for 30 minutes.

Place the pork and half the marinade into a baking tray with the butter and cover it with the banana leaf. Cover the tray with aluminum foil and bake for 30 minutes. Remove from the oven and pull the meat off the bone. Add a little of the marinade to the pulled pork if you wish.

Heat tortillas in the oven for 1–2 minutes. Alternatively, heat a frypan and add the tortillas, one at a time. Cook for 1–2 minutes each side. Keep warm while you heat the rest of the tortillas.

Serve the pork hot on the tortillas with salsa habanero.

Note: Achiote is used extensively in Mexican cooking to add color and flavor. Made from annatto seeds, it is sometimes called the 'saffron of Mexico'. The flavor is described as being a very mild nutty, musky and earthy. It may be difficult to get (try online). If you can't source it, a good substitute is turmeric or paprika or a mixture of both.

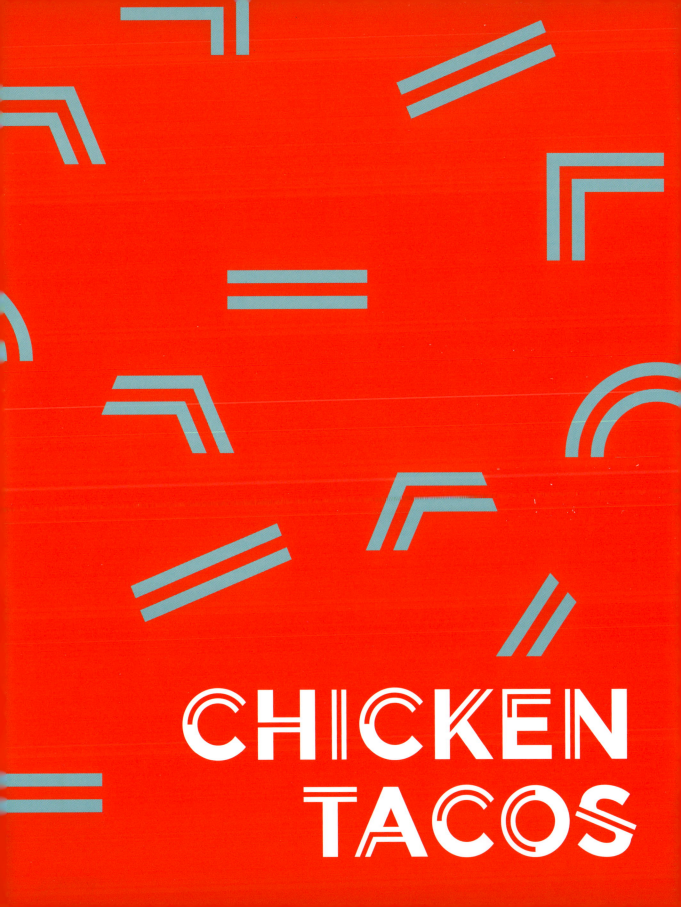

CHICKEN ALAMBRE TACOS

SERVES 4

- 4 chicken thighs, skinless and boneless
- 3 tablespoons vegetable oil
- 340 g (12 oz) green capsicum (bell pepper), julienne
- 340 g (12 oz) yellow capsicum (bell pepper), julienne
- 300 g (10½ oz) onion, julienne
- 500 ml (16 fl oz) dark beer (dark lager, brown ale or stout)
- 1–2 teaspoons salt
- 150 g (5¼ oz) cheese, grated
- 4 corn flour tortillas
- Green sauce, to taste (see sauces)

Rinse the chicken thoroughly and pat dry with paper towel or clean cloth. Cut the chicken into strips.

Heat the oil in a frypan and add the thighs, capsicum and onion. Stir constantly to make sure it cooks evenly, about 2 minutes. Pour in the beer and season with salt.

Continue cooking until the liquid is reduced by half. Stir in the cheese then remove from the heat.

Heat tortillas in the oven for 1–2 minutes. Alternatively, heat a frypan and add the tortillas, one at a time. Cook for 1–2 minutes each side. Keep warm while you heat the rest of the tortillas.

Serve the chicken over the hot tortillas with green sauce.

CHICKEN TACOS

CHICKEN SALPICON TACOS

SERVES 4

- 600 g (21 oz) chicken breast
- 600 ml (20 fl oz) water
- 20 g (¾ oz) sea salt
- 1 romaine lettuce
- 400 g (14 oz) ripe tomatoes, roughly chopped
- 125 g (4 ½ oz) white onion, roughly chopped
- 100 g (3½ oz) serrano chili
- 200 g (7 oz) avocado, cut into cubes
- 1–2 teaspoons salt
- 120 ml (4¼ fl oz) olive oil
- 4 corn flour tortillas

Note: Salpicon in Spanish means 'medley' or 'hodgepodge'. In Mexican cooking, it refers to a salad mix that includes chili, tomato and avocado.

Wash and thoroughly dry chicken breast with paper towel or clean cloth.

In a saucepan, add the water, salt and chicken. Bring to the boil and reduce heat. Cook covered/uncovered for 30 minutes.

Remove the chicken from the broth and cool. Shred the chicken and place in a bowl. Reserve the broth for other recipes if you wish.

Wash the salad vegetables thoroughly and dry.

Cut the lettuce into wide strips. Place in a bowl with tomatoes, onion, chili and avocado. Add the shredded chicken, olive oil and season with salt.

Heat tortillas in the oven for 1–2 minutes. Alternatively, heat a frypan and add the tortillas, one at a time. Cook for 1–2 minutes each side. Keep warm while you heat the rest of the tortillas.

Serve the chicken and salad over the hot tortillas.

CHICKEN POBLANO CHILI AND CORN TACOS

SERVES 4

- 4 chicken legs, skinless and boneless
- 800 ml (27½ fl oz) water
- 1 white onion, roughly cut into pieces
- 1 garlic, whole
- 400 g (14 oz) fresh poblano chili
- 200 g (7 oz) canned corn, chopped
- salt, to taste
- ground white pepper, to taste
- 220 g (7¾ oz) sour cream
- 4 corn tortillas

Note: Poblano chilies are mild to medium in heat. One of the most commonly used chilies in Central Mexican cooking, they are used fresh and dried (dried poblanos are also called ancho chilies. If you can't find them, substitute with a mild chili such as jalapeño.

Cook the chicken in water with salt, onion and garlic for 45 minutes. Remove the chicken, let it cool and cut into small cubes. Reserve broth.

Grind the poblano chili in a mortar and pestle to remove the skin. It will begin to detach then use your fingers to continue removing the skin. Cut into julienne.

In a saucepan, add a little of the chicken broth, the chicken, slices of poblano, chopped corn and cream. Bring to the boil, reduce heat and cook on low for 10 minutes.

Heat tortillas in the oven for 1–2 minutes. Alternatively, heat a frypan and add the tortillas, one at a time. Cook for 1–2 minutes each side. Keep warm while you heat the rest of the tortillas.

Serve the chicken and chili over hot corn tortillas.

CHICKEN TACOS

GRILLED CHICKEN TACOS

SERVES 4

- 2 chicken legs, skinless and boneless
- 2 chicken thighs, skinless and boneless
- 250 ml (8 oz) light beer (such as Pale Ale or Pale Lager)
- 100 g (3½ oz) red onion, sliced
- pinch of salt
- 20 ml (⅔ fl oz) vegetable oil
- 4 wheat flour tortillas
- 1 cup coriander (cilantro), roughly chopped
- 160 g (5½ oz) Pico de Gallo (see sauces)

Rinse the chicken thoroughly and pat dry with a paper towel or a clean cloth.

In a bowl, add the beer, salt and onion and mix well.

Add the chicken to the bowl and make sure all pieces are well covered with the mixture. Place in the refrigerator for 3 hours.

On a grill over medium heat add the oil and distribute evenly. Increase the temperature to hot and add the chicken. Cook until brown on one side then turn and cook on the other to brown.

Ladle some of the liquid from the marinade over the chicken from time to time to prevent it from drying out. When the chicken is cooked through, about 8–10 minutes, remove from the grill. Cool slightly and cut into strips.

Heat tortillas in the oven for 1–2 minutes. Alternatively, heat a frypan and add the tortillas, one at a time. Cook for 1–2 minutes each side. Keep warm while you heat the rest of the tortillas.

Serve the chicken and tinga over the hot tortillas with chopped coriander and pico de gallo.

CHICKEN TACOS

MULATO CHICKEN TACOS

SERVES 4

- 4 chicken thighs, skinless and boneless
- 1½ L (50 fl oz) water
- 1 white onion
- 1 garlic clove
- 4 mulato chilies, seeded
- 50 g (1¾ oz) walnut
- 2 tablespoons vegetable oil
- 150 ml (5 fl oz) fresh cream
- salt, to taste
- 4 large corn tortillas

Note: Mulato chilies are mild to medium dried chilies that are most often used in Mexican mole sauces. Ranked very low on the heat scale, they have a soft smoky flavor with a taste similar to chocolate and licorice. Substitute with ancho chiles or if you can't source these either, cayenne pepper.

Cut each chicken thigh into 6 pieces.

Add water to a large saucepan. Add the chicken, onion, garlic and salt. Bring to the boil, reduce and cook for 30 minutes. Remove the chicken from the broth and allow to cool. Strain the broth, reserving both onion and garlic (and the broth for other recipes if desired).

To make the mulatto sauce, wash chilies, roast them and then soaked in hot water for 20 minutes.

In a blender, grind the chilies and walnuts with garlic and onion from the chicken broth to make a paste.

Heat a saucepan with the oil. Add the paste, season with salt and cook over a medium low heat for 5 minutes.

Add the chicken to the sauce and cook for 5 minutes.

Heat tortillas in the oven for 1–2 minutes. Alternatively, heat a frypan and add the tortillas, one at a time. Cook for 1–2 minutes each side. Keep warm while you heat the rest of the tortillas.

Serve over the hot tortillas.

CHICKEN TACOS

CRUMBED CHICKEN TACOS

SERVES 4

- 800 g (1 lb 10 oz) chicken breasts
- salt, to taste
- 250 g (8¾ oz) plain (all purpose) flour
- 4 eggs, lightly beaten
- 300 g (10½ oz) dry breadcrumbs
- vegetable oil, for frying
- salt, to taste
- 4 large wheat tortillas
- iceberg lettuce, washed, dried and shredded
- Guacamole (see sauces)

Fillet the chicken breasts into four servings. Pat dry with paper towel or clean cloth. Season with salt.

Put the flour on one plate, the egg in a bowl and breadcrumbs on another plate. Coat the chicken with flour, coat with the beaten egg and roll in the breadcrumbs to coat completely.

In a deep fryer or saucepan, heat enough oil that will allow the chicken to submerge. When hot, and fry the chicken fillets one or two at a time depending on the size of your fryer. Fry for 6–8 minutes or until golden brown. Drain on a wire rack.

Heat tortillas in the oven for 1–2 minutes. Alternatively, heat a frypan and add the tortillas, one at a time. Cook for 1–2 minutes each side. Keep warm while you heat the rest of the tortillas.

To serve, slice chicken breasts into thick strips and place on the hot tortillas. Add the lettuce and guacamole on top of the chicken.

CHICKEN TACOS

CHICKEN ONION JALAPEÑO TACOS

SERVES 4

- 40 ml (1½ fl oz) vegetable oil
- 3 large onions, cut julienne
- 100 g (3½ oz) fresh jalapeño peppers, sliced
- 500 g (17½ oz) chicken breast, cut into strips
- salt, to taste
- ground black pepper, to taste
- 4 corn tortillas
- 1–2 avocados, cut into wedges, to serve
- Red sauce (see sauce), to serve

Add vegetable oil to a hot frypan. Add the onion, jalapeño pepper and brown for 4 minutes stirring constantly.

Stir in the strips of chicken. Season with salt and pepper. Fry for 6–7 minutes or until the chicken is cooked through.

Heat tortillas in the oven for 1–2 minutes. Alternatively, heat a frypan and add the tortillas, one at a time. Cook for 1–2 minutes each side. Keep warm while you heat the rest of the tortillas.

Serve the chicken on hot tortillas with avocado and red sauce.

CHICKEN AND APPLE TACOS

SERVES 4

- 600 g (21 oz) chicken breast
- salt and pepper, to taste
- 1½ tablespoons butter
- 1½ tablespoons olive oil
- 600 ml (20 fl oz) fresh apple juice
- aromatic herbs (1 teaspoon dried oregano, ¼ teaspoon ground cloves, 1 teaspoon cumin, 1 cinnamon stick, 2 bay leaves, 1 teaspoon paprika)
- 4 wheat flour tortillas
- 1 lemon, juiced
- ½ bunch coriander (cilantro), chopped
- 1 onion, chopped
- Tamaulipas Sauce (see sauces)

Rinse and pat dry the chicken with paper towel or a dry cloth. Cut into bite-sized pieces. Season with salt and pepper.

Heat a shallow frypan and add the butter and oil. Add the chicken pieces and fry for a couple of minutes until chicken is lightly golden.

Pour in the apple juice and add assorted herbs. Cook the chicken in the apple juice until the liquid reduces by half.

Heat tortillas in the oven for 1–2 minutes. Alternatively, heat a frypan and add the tortillas, one at a time. Cook for 1–2 minutes each side. Keep warm while you heat the rest of the tortillas.

With a slotted spoon, remove the chicken and serve on the hot tortillas. Add lemon juice, coriander, onion and the tamaulipas sauce to taste.

CHICKEN TACOS

CHICKEN TINGA TACOS

SERVES 4

- 750 g (1 lb 8 oz) chicken breast
- 1 L (2 pt) water
- 2 teaspoons sea salt
- 1 brown onion, roughly chopped
- 2 garlic cloves, peeled
- 300 g (10½ oz) ripe tomatoes
- 140 g (5 oz) chipotle peppers, chopped
- 1 garlic clove, chopped
- 1 white onion, cut julienne
- 4 corn tortillas

In a large saucepan, add the chicken breast with water, salt, brown onion and garlic. Bring to the boil, reduce to a rolling simmer, partially cover with a lid and cook for 45 minutes to make a broth. Remove lid and allow to cool. Remove chicken and place in a bowl. Strain the stock and retain.

Roast the tomatoes on the barbecue or a gas hot plate over low heat until the skin is charred. Cool and finely chop.

In a saucepan, add the tomato, chipotle, chicken broth and garlic and blend to a thick sauce. Cool and add to a blender to form a smooth sauce.

In a saucepan mix the chicken, white onion and sauce. Cook over a low heat until the onion is soft.

Heat tortillas in the oven for 1–2 minutes. Alternatively, heat a frypan and add the tortillas, one at a time. Cook for 1–2 minutes each side. Keep warm while you heat the rest of the tortillas.

Serve the chicken in tinga sauce on hot tortillas.

SHRIMP TACOS

SERVES 4

- 500 g (17½ oz) medium uncooked shrimp (green prawns)
- salt and pepper, to taste
- 2 tablespoons vegetable oil
- 1 tablespoon butter
- 4 corn tortillas
- 1 tablespoon butter, melted
- Red sauce (see sauces)
- ½ bunch coriander (cilantro), roughly chopped

Peel, remove the head and devein the shrimp. Season with salt and pepper to taste

Heat a non-stick frypan with the butter and oil. Add shrimp and sauté for about 4 minutes until cooked. Drain on paper towels.

Heat tortillas in the oven for 1–2 minutes. Alternatively, heat a frypan and add the tortillas, one at a time. Cook for 1–2 minutes each side. Keep warm while you heat the rest of the tortillas.

Serve shrimp on hot tortillas. Pour over the melted butter. Add red sauce and sprinkle with cilantro.

SEAFOOD TACOS

FRIED FISH TACOS

SERVES 4

- 500 g (17½ oz) fish fillet
- 4 tablespoons plain (all purpose) flour
- 3 eggs, lightly beaten
- 500 ml (16 fl oz) vegetable oil, for frying
- 4 corn tortillas
- 1 medium white onion
- 20 g (3/4 oz) chipotle chilies
- 30 g (1 oz) cabbage
- 30 g (1 oz) carrot
- 1 lemon, juiced
- Guacamole (see sauces)

Note: Fish have different names depending on where you live. The best fish for tacos is any boneless firm fish such as tilapia, halibut, mahi mahi, swordfish, salmon, gem fish (hake), cod, bass, haddock and snapper to name a few.

Pat dry the fish with paper towel or clean cloth.

Put flour on a plate and egg in a bowl. Roll the fish in flour to cover, then dip into the egg making sure the egg coats the whole fillet.

Heat oil in a deep fryer or large saucepan.
The oil needs to be hot enough that the fillets sizzle when added.

Fry fish for 3 minutes or until the fish is golden brown. Do not overload the fryer as the oil will lose heat. Fry in batches if necessary to ensure the oil stays hot. Drain fish on a wire rack. Cool and cut into strips and set aside.

Wash and dry the chilies, cabbage and carrots.

Peel the onion and finely slice. Cut the chili, cabbage and carrot julienne (very thin sticks). julienne. Mix them all together and place in a bowl.

Heat tortillas in the oven for 1–2 minutes. Alternatively, heat a frypan and add the tortillas, one at a time. Cook for 1–2 minutes each side. Keep warm while you heat the rest of the tortillas.

Serve the fish over the tortillas with the salad and guacamole.

SEAFOOD TACOS

SHRIMP COCONUT TACOS

SERVES 4

- 200 g (7 oz) plain (all purpose) flour
- 2 eggs, lightly beaten
- ½–1 tablespoon milk
- pinch of salt
- 250 g (8¾ oz) corn flakes
- 250 g (8¾ oz) shredded coconut
- 12 large uncooked shrimp (green prawns)
- 80 ml (2¾ fl oz) lemon juice
- salt, to taste
- 500 ml (16 fl oz) vegetable oil, for frying
- Guacamole (see sauces), to serve

Note: Corn flakes can be substituted with dry breadcrumbs, panko crumbs or quinoa flakes.

To make the batter for shrimp, in a bowl add flour, egg, milk and salt. Whisk until a batter forms. Set aside.

To make the coating, lay out some baking paper and use a rolling pin to grind the corn flakes so they resemble dry breadcrumbs. Mix with shredded coconut.

Peel, remove the head and devein the shrimp and rinse under cold water. Pat dry with paper towel or a dry clean cloth.

Dip shrimp in the lemon juice, then into the batter mix and roll in the cornflakes and coconut mix to coat thoroughly. Put shrimp on a plate, cover and place in the refrigerator for up to 1 hour.

Heat the oil in a deep fryer or large saucepan. The oil needs to be hot enough that the shrimp sizzle when added. Fry for 3 minutes or until the shrimp are golden brown. Do not overload the fryer as the oil will lose heat. Fry in batches if necessary to ensure the oil stays hot. Drain on a wire rack.

Heat tortillas in the oven for 1–2 minutes. Alternatively, heat a frypan and add the tortillas, one at a time. Cook for 1–2 minutes each side. Keep warm while you heat the rest of the tortillas.

Serve the shrimp on the hot corn tortillas with guacamole.

SEAFOOD TACOS

CRAB TACOS

SERVES 4

- 300 g (10½ oz) crab meat
- 2 tomatoes, chopped
- 2 tablespoons parsley, chopped
- 2 red chilies, sliced
- 4 tablespoons lemon juice
- 3 tablespoons tomato sauce (ketchup)
- 2 tablespoons mayonnaise
- 4 wheat flour tortillas served hot
- 1 avocado, peeled and chopped, to serve

Mix the crab meat with tomatoes, parsley, chili, lemon juice and tomato sauce. Cover and place in the refrigerator for 30 minutes.

Stir crab meat mixture and remove all liquid that has formed. Add salt.

Spread some mayonnaise on each tortilla then spread the crab mixture and top with avocado.

SEAFOOD TACOS

FISH WITH ORANGE TACOS

- 4 fish fillets
- 440 ml (15 fl oz) water
- 1 tablespoon lemon juice
- salt, to taste
- 1½ tablespoons olive oil
- 240 ml (8 fl oz) orange juice
- 100 ml (3½ fl oz) white wine
- 2 teaspoons cornflour (corn starch)
- salt, to taste
- 4 large corn tortillas
- Green sauce (see sauces), to serve

Note: The best fish for tacos is any boneless firm fish such as tilapia, halibut, mahi mahi, swordfish, gem fish (hake), cod, bass, haddock or snapper to name a few.

Soak the fish in the water with the lemon juice for 5 minutes. Remove, drain and dry with paper towel or a dry, clean cloth. Season with salt.

Heat the oil in a shallow frypan. Add the fillets. Sauté over medium heat for 10 minutes. Remove from heat and set aside.

In a bowl mix the orange juice with the wine, corn flour and a little salt. Add to the fish.

Return to the heat, covered and cook over low heat until the fish is cooked.

Heat tortillas in the oven for 1–2 minutes. Alternatively, heat a frypan and add the tortillas, one at a time. Cook for 1–2 minutes each side. Keep warm while you heat the rest of the tortillas.

Serve the fish and orange sauce over hot tortillas with the green salsa.

SEAFOOD TACOS

DIABLA SHIMP WITH CHEESE TACOS

SERVES 4

- 8 guajillo chilies
- 220 ml (7 fl oz) olive oil
- 8 garlic cloves, chopped
- 800 g (1lb 10 oz) large shrimp (green prawns), peeled and deveined
- salt, to taste
- 1 tablespoon parsley, chopped
- 300 g (10½ oz) Manchego cheese, grated
- 4 large flour tortillas
- 200 g (7 oz) avocado, cut into wedges, to serve

Note: Substitute guajillo chili with any other mild to medium hot chili. Substitute Manchego cheese with Pecorino Romano or even cheddar, Gruyère or a Monterey Jack.

Clean the chilies and cut them in julienne.

Heat the olive oil in a frypan and sauté the garlic over medium heat until golden.

Add the chili and cook until the oil begins to turn red.

Remove the heads from the shrimp and add to the pan. Season with salt and cook for 5 minutes over medium heat.

Remove the pan from the heat and sprinkle with parsley and the cheese. Stir in gently until the cheese melts.

Heat tortillas in the oven for 1–2 minutes. Alternatively, heat a frypan and add the tortillas, one at a time. Cook for 1–2 minutes each side. Keep warm while you heat the rest of the tortillas.

Serve hot on tortillas with avocado wedges.

SEAFOOD TACOS

MEXICAN OCTOPUS TACOS

SERVES 4

- 1 kg (2.2 lb) octopus
- water, to cover
- 45 ml (1½ fl oz) vegetable oil
- 200 g (7 oz) onion, chopped
- 1 garlic clove, chopped
- 1 bay leaf
- ½ teaspoon thyme
- ½ teaspoon marjoram
- 8 Serrano peppers, chopped
- 8 tomatoes, skin removed, seeded and chopped
- 15 black olives, chopped
- 4 wheat flour tortillas

Note: Serrano peppers get their name from the area of Mexico where they originated, the states of Puebla and Hidalgo. They are hotter than the more well known Jalapeno pepper which is the best substitute if you cannot source serrano peppers.

Wash the octopus and pat dry with paper towel or a clean cloth. Remove the beak.

Half fill a heavy-based saucepan with water and bring to the boil. Slowly lower the octopus into the water so that the legs curl as they are being lowered. Bring back to the boil, lower heat to medium and cover. Cook for 45 minutes. Turn heat to high then reduce to low and cook 10 minutes. Turn off heat and let pressure release naturally.

Remove the octopus from the pot and while still warm, rub the skin on the legs to remove. Cut into 2 cm (3/4 in) pieces.

Heat the oil in a frypan and sauté the onion and garlic. Add the octopus, bay leaf, thyme and marjoram and cook for 5 minutes.

Add the peppers, tomatoes and olives and cook for another 10–15 minutes until the tomatoes are cooked through. Season to taste.

Heat tortillas in the oven for 1–2 minutes. Alternatively, heat a frypan and add the tortillas, one at a time. Cook for 1–2 minutes each side. Keep warm while you heat the rest of the tortillas.

Serve octopus hot over wheat flour tortillas.

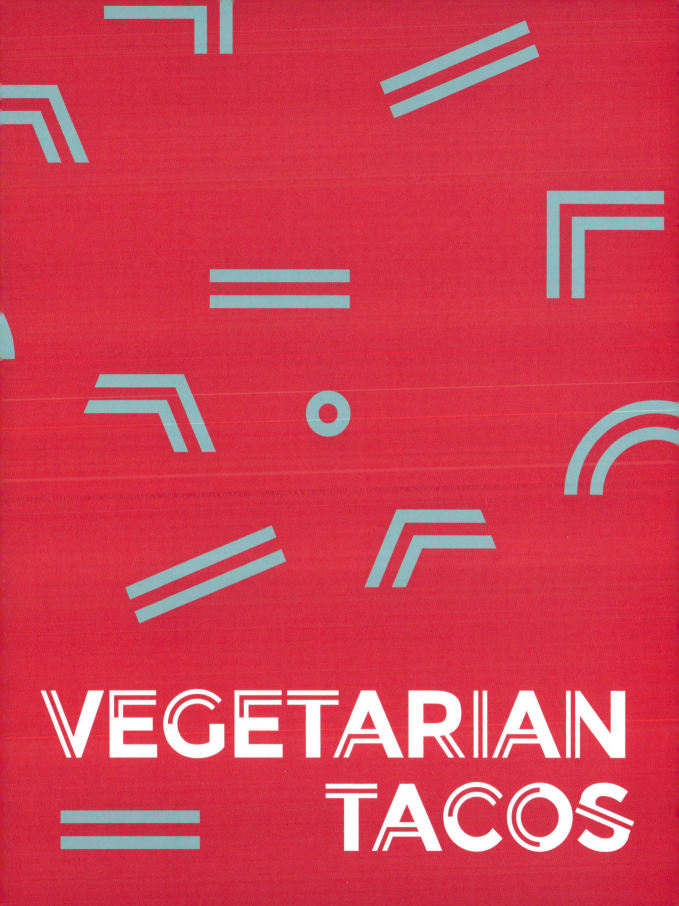

VEGETARIAN TACOS

MUSHROOMS, ZUCCHINI AND SPINACH TACOS

SERVES 4

- 25 ml (¾ oz) olive oil
- 55 g (1¾ oz) onion, chopped
- 2 garlic cloves, chopped
- 200 g (7 oz) zucchini, washed and sliced
- 500 g (17½ oz) mushrooms, sliced
- 100 g (3 ½ oz) spinach, washed and finely chopped
- 200 g (7 oz) manchego cheese
- 4 corn tortillas
- Red sauce (see sauces)

Heat the oil in a frypan and sauté the onion and garlic until the onion is translucent.

Add zucchini and continue cooking on low heat for 5 minutes.

Add the mushrooms and spinach and cook until the mushrooms are soft.

Add the cheese and stir in to melt. Remove from heat.

Heat tortillas in the oven for 1–2 minutes. Alternatively, heat a frypan and add the tortillas, one at a time. Cook for 1–2 minutes each side. Keep warm while you heat the rest of the tortillas.

Serve on hot tortillas with the red sauce.

Note: Manchego cheese from Le Mancha in Spain and is traditionally made from unpasteurized goat's milk. If you cannot find, substitute with Pecorino Romano or even cheddar, Gruyère or a Monterey Jack.

VEGETARIAN TACOS

BEAN AND SPINACH TACOS

SERVES 4

- 1 tablespoon olive oil
- 50 g (1¾ oz) onion, chopped
- 1 garlic clove, chopped
- 200 g (7 oz) spinach
- 2 tomatoes, skin removed, deseeded and cut into cubes
- 300 g (10½ oz) canned cannellini beans, rinsed and drained
- 4 corn tortillas
- 120 g (4¼ oz) avocado, sliced, to serve
- 100 g (3½ oz) cheddar shredded cheese, to serve

In a hot frypan, add the oil and sauté the onion and garlic until onion is translucent.

Add the spinach and tomatoes and cook over medium heat for 5 minutes.

Add beans and continue to cook for 4 more minutes.

Heat tortillas in the oven for 1–2 minutes. Alternatively, heat a frypan and add the tortillas, one at a time. Cook for 1–2 minutes each side. Keep warm while you heat the rest of the tortillas.

Serve over the hot tortillas with avocado and cheese.

VEGETARIAN TACOS

PICO DE GALLO AND AVOCADO TACOS

SERVES 4

- 250 g (9 oz) tomatoes, seeded and diced
- 100 g (3½ oz) onion, chopped
- 250 g (9 oz) avocado, cubed
- 50 g (1¾ oz) coriander (cilantro), chopped
- 25 ml (¾ fl oz) lemon juice
- 100 g (3½) panela cheese, cubed
- salt, to taste
- 4 corn tortillas

In a bowl, mix the tomato, onion, avocado, coriander, lemon juice and cheese. Season with salt.

Heat tortillas in the oven for 1–2 minutes. Alternatively, heat a frypan and add the tortillas, one at a time. Cook for 1–2 minutes each side. Keep warm while you heat the rest of the tortillas.

Serve over the hot tortillas.

Note: Panela cheese can be substituted with ricotta.

VEGETARIAN TACOS

GRILLED NOPALES TACOS

SERVES 4

- 100 g (3½ oz) onion, finely sliced
- 2 red tomatoes, seeded and chopped
- 20 g (¾ oz) coriander (cilantro)
- 40 ml (1⅓ fl oz) lemon juice
- salt and pepper, to taste
- 12 baby nopales
- 4 lettuce leaves
- 1 avocado, peeled and cut into wedges
- 8 cherry tomatoes, cut into quarters
- 80 g (2¾ oz) panela cheese, crumbled
- 4 wheat flour tortillas

In a bowl mix onion, tomatoes, coriander and lemon juice. Season with salt and pepper. Set the salad aside for at least 30 minutes.

Season the nopales with salt and pepper and roast them on a barbecue hot plate (or in a frypan). Cook on both sides for 10 minutes. Set aside.

Heat tortillas in the oven for 1–2 minutes. Alternatively, heat a frypan and add the tortillas, one at a time. Cook for 1–2 minutes each side. Keep warm while you heat the rest of the tortillas.

To serve, place a lettuce leaf on the tortilla. On top of the lettuce, add the nopales, avocado, cherry tomatoes and cheese. Finish with a little of the onion, tomato and coriander salad.

Note: Panela cheese (queso panela) is a white, smooth cheese from Mexico made of pasteurized cow's milk. If unavailable, substitute with ricotta.

VEGETARIAN TACOS

MUSHROOMS WITH GUAJILLO SAUCE

SERVES 4

- 4 red tomatoes, whole
- 3 guajillo peppers, deseeded
- 2 chipotle peppers
- 160 ml (5½ fl oz) water
- 1 tablespoon vegetable oil
- 200 g (7 oz) onion, chopped
- 2 garlic cloves, minced
- 500 g (17½ oz) mushrooms, chopped
- 1 teaspoon epazote, chopped
- salt and pepper, to taste
- 4 wheat flour tortillas

In a griddle or large frypan, roast the tomatoes and the guajillos for 30 minutes. Remove from heat and cool. Add to a blender and liquefy with the chipotles and enough water to form a sauce.

Add the sauce to a frypan and sauté over low heat until it comes to a boil. Season with salt and pepper. Remove from heat and set aside.

In another frypan, heat the oil and sauté the onion and garlic until the onion is translucent.

Add the mushrooms and epazote. Season with salt and pepper and cook over low heat.

Add the sauce and cook until liquid reduces by 50 per cent.

Heat tortillas in the oven for 1–2 minutes. Alternatively, heat a frypan and add the tortillas, one at a time. Cook for 1–2 minutes each side. Keep warm while you heat the rest of the tortillas.

Serve the mushrooms on the hot tortillas.

Note: Epazote is a herb used in the cuisines of central and southern Mexico and Guatemala. It has a pungent flavor with hints of oregano, anise, citrus, mint, and even tar. If you can't source it fresh, dried epazote can be found at specialty herb shops or online.

VEGETARIAN TACOS

RAJAS POBLANAS WITH SOUR CREAM

SERVES 4

- 1½ tablespoons vegetable oil
- 60 g (2 oz) butter
- 80 g (2¾ oz) onion, finely sliced
- 320 g (11¼ oz) corn kernels
- 500 g (17 ½ oz) poblano chilies
- 300 ml (10 fl oz) sour cream
- salt, to taste
- 4 corn tortillas

To a hot frypan add butter and oil. Add the onion and stir. Cook until the onion is translucent.

Add the corn and keep stirring for 15 minutes. Leave for 10 minutes to cool down.

Blister the skin of the chilies over a flame. Cool and remove the skin. Remove seeds and cut into thick slices. Add to the pan, stir and cook for 20 minutes until soft.

Add the sour cream, bring just to the boil, reduce heat and cook over low heat for 5 minutes. Season with salt.

Heat tortillas in the oven for 1–2 minutes. Alternatively, heat a frypan and add the tortillas, one at a time. Cook for 1–2 minutes each side. Keep warm while you heat the rest of the tortillas.

Serve over the hot tortillas.

Note: Rajas Poblanas is so named as 'rajas' means slices and the dish is made mainly of slices of Poblano peppers (or Chiles Poblanos) which are quite mild in terms of heat but full of flavor. If you can't find them, you can substitute with capsicum (bell peppers) which are milder or serrano peppers which are hotter.

VEGETARIAN TACOS

PEPPERS WITH CHEESE TACOS

SERVES 4

- 1–2 tablespoons olive oil
- 100 g (3½ oz) white onion, finely sliced
- 100 g (3½ oz) red onion, finely sliced
- 2 garlic cloves, chopped
- 1 green capsicum (bell pepper), finely sliced
- 1 yellow capsicum (bell pepper), finely sliced
- 1 red capsicum (bell pepper), finely sliced
- ½ teaspoon ground cumin
- 200 g (6¾ oz) Oaxaca cheese, cut into strips
- 4 corn or wheat tortillas
- salt and pepper to taste
- 1 lemon, cut into wedges, to serve
- Guacamole (see sauces), to serve

Heat oil in a frypan. Add the onion, garlic and peppers. Cook over medium heat 10 minutes mixing from time to time to cook evenly. Cook until onions and capsicum have softened but still feel firm. Season with cumin, salt and pepper.

Add the Oaxaca cheese. Remove from the heat and allow the cheese to melt.

Heat tortillas in the oven for 1–2 minutes. Alternatively, heat a frypan and add the tortillas, one at a time. Cook for 1–2 minutes each side. Keep warm while you heat the rest of the tortillas.

Serve over the tortillas with lemon wedges and guacamole.

Note: If Oaxaca cheese is unavailable, substitute with a mozzarella-like string cheese.

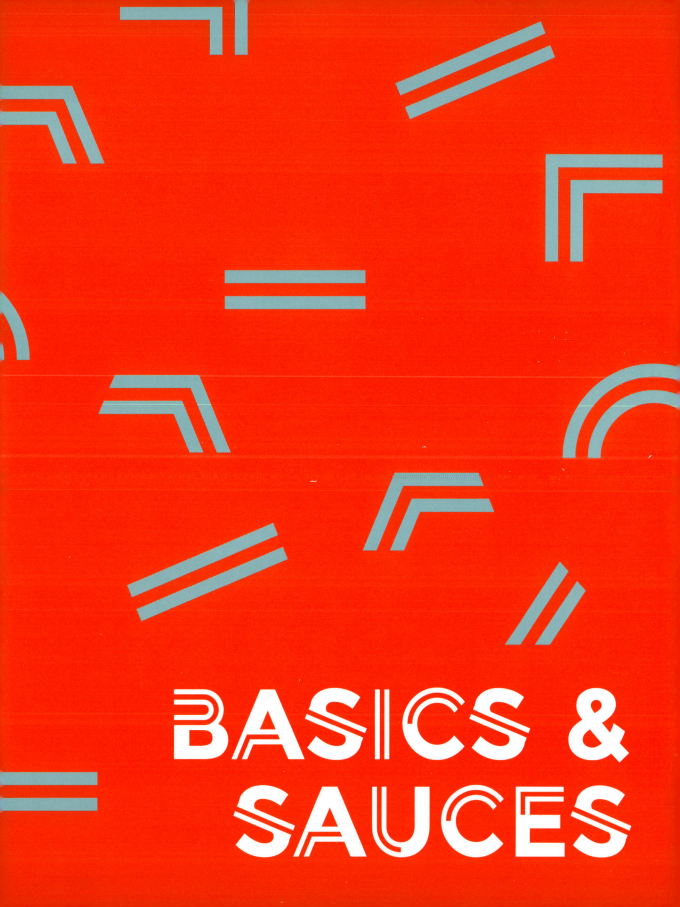

BASICS & SAUCES

HOMEMADE TORTILLAS

- 2 cups masa harina
- ½ spoon of salt
- 1½ cups of hot tap water

Note: To make our corn tortillas we need Masa Harina. This is a ground from corn kernels that have being soaked in water with lime. This solution changes the structure of the corn, making it softer and with a great nutrional content.

Create the dough by mixing the masa harina and the salt in a bowl. Add the water slowly and stir for few minutes. Massage the dough using your hands, massage the dough for 2 minutes in a mixing bowl until smooth. Give the masa time to absorb the water. If you want a better result rest the dough for 30 minutes.

When you feel the dough is smooth then it is ready and you can then start creating balls in your hands. Mould the balls to about the size of a golf ball, this will create a 15¼ cm (6-in) tortilla, depending on the size of the tortillas you would like you can make bigger or smaller balls.

To press the dough you can either use a tortilla press, or a rolling pin. The tortilla press will make it easier to make round tortillas however you can also press the dough underneath a heavy skillet for the shape.

Cook the tortillas for 70 seconds, until the edges are starting to curl up and the bottoms look dry and pebbly, then flip it over and do the same to the other side.

Place the tortillas straight under a tea towel or in a warm place to keep them warm until you need them.

BASICS & SAUCES

GUACAMOLE

- 500 g (17½ oz) avocado
- 100 g (3½ oz) white onion, finely chopped
- 3 serranos chilies, finely chopped
- 2 ½ tablespoons coriander (cilantro), chopped
- 5 lemons, juiced
- 20 g (3/4 oz) sour cream
- ½ teaspoon salt

Cut the avocados in half and remove the pit. Spoon the flesh of the avocado into a large bowl and mash with a fork.

Mix in the onion, chilies, coriander and lemons. Add the cream and salt.

Note: Homemade guacamole can last up to 2 days in the refrigerator. Covering the surface with extra lemon juice will help it retain its color.

BASICS & SAUCES

CHILLED ONIONS

- 40 ml (1⅓ fl oz) vegetable oil
- 500 g 17½ oz) white onion, finely sliced
- 30 g (1 oz) chipotle chilies
- water, as required
- salt and pepper, to taste

Add the oil to a frypan and heat. Sauté the onion and sauté for 4 minutes.

Add chipotle chilies to a mortar and with pestle grind to a paste. Add water to lightly dilute if necessary.

Add the chipotle to the frypan and continue to cook for 5 minutes making sure the onion does not take up the color of chilopte.

Season and turn off the heat. Allow to cool.

Store the sauce in an air-tight container until ready to serve.

Note: This sauce can last up to 4 days in the refrigerator and 30 days in the freezer.

ROASTED TOMATOES

- 8 large tomatoes
- sea salt, to taste
- vegetable oil, to cook

Blister the skin of the tomatoes on a flat grill or frypan on high heat with a little vegetable oil. Rotate the tomatoes until skins blackened.

Add sea salt to taste.

Note: This sauce can last up to 1 week in the refrigerator.

SOUR TOMATOES

- 10–12 small green tomatoes (stems removed, tomatoes should be firm)
- ½ cup salt
- 1 cup white vinegar
- ½ cup corriander seeds
- 6–8 crushed garlic cloves
- 3 teaspoons chili pepper flakes
- ½ cup white sugar

Heat all of the ingredients, except the tomatoes in a pot; bring to a high heat, but not a boil. Set aside.

In jars, or airtight containers, place the small or halfed tomatoes, add the brine, and seal. All tomatoes must be fully covered.

Note: This sauce can last up to 3 months in the refrigerator.

SALSA ROJA

- 20 g (3/4 oz) chillies tree
- 20 g (3/4 oz) Guajillo chili
- 500 g (17½ oz) red tomatoes
- 150 g (5 oz) green tomatoes
- 1½ tablespoons vegetable oil
- 2 garlic cloves
- 150 g (5 oz) white onion
- 800 ml (27 fl oz) water
- salt, to taste

Wash the tomatoes and chilis and dry.

Add the oil to a frypan. When oil is hot, add the chilies, tomatoes, garlic and onion. Roast all ingredients until they take on a slight dark color without burning them.

Add water to the frying pan, and let cook for 10 minutes. Turn off the heat, pour into a bowl and allow to cool.

Place the ingredients in a food processor with the salt and blend to form a sauce. Strain.

Store in an air-tight container until ready to serve.

Note: Salsa Roja is also called red sauce.

SALSA VERDE

- 1.L (2 pt) water
- 500 g (17 ½ oz) green tomatoes
- 1½ tablespoons serranos chilies
- 75 g (2 ½ oz) avocado
- 200 g (7 oz) white onion
- 2 garlic cloves
- 1 lemon
- ½ teaspoon salt

Wash and dry the tomatoes and chilies.

Add the tomato, chilies, white onion and garlic in a saucepan. Add enough water to cover.

Bring to the boil, reduce temperature and cook over medium heat for 5 minutes. Remove from the heat, place in a bowl and allow to cool.

Place the ingredients in a food processor with avocado, lemon juice and salt. Blend to form a sauce. Strain and adjust seasoning as required.

Store the sauce in an air-tight container until ready to serve.

Note: This is also called green sauce. It can be stored in an air-tight container in the refrigerator for up to 2 months.

BASICS & SAUCES

SALSA HABANERO

- 1 Spanish onion, finely sliced
- 150 ml (5 fl oz) apple cider vinegar
- ½ teaspoon oregano
- ½ teaspoon salt
- 50 g (1¾ oz) habanero chilies
- 130 g (4¾ oz) diced mango

Place the sliced Spanish onion, apple cider vinegar, oregano and salt into a bowl and stir.

Clean the habanero chilies, making sure you remove the seeds, then cut them into thin strips.

Add the chilies and the mango to the mix.

Let it stand for 1 hour then check the seasoning.

Store in an air tight container in the refrigerator until needed.

Note: Habanero chillies (peppers) are amongst the hottest in the world. This sauce is for those who love the heat but if you don't, beware.

BASICS & SAUCES

SALSA TAMAULIPAS

- 80 g (2¾ oz) dried tree chilies, halved
- 500 g (17½ oz) ripe tomatoes, halved
- 250 g (8¾ oz) green tomato, halved
- 1–2 tablespoons vegetable oil
- 5 garlic cloves, roughly chopped
- 200 g (7 oz) white onion, roughly chopped
- 500 ml (16 fl oz) water
- ½ teaspoon salt

Wash and dry the chilies and tomato.

Add the oil to a frypan and heat.

Add the chilies, tomatoes, green tomatoes, garlic and onion and cook until all ingredients take on a slightly darker color without burning.

Add water to the pan and cook for 10 minutes. Season and turn off the heat. Place the sauce in a bowl and allow to cool.

Place the ingredients in a food processor with avocado, lemon juice and salt. Blend to form a sauce. Strain and adjust seasoning as required.

Store the sauce in an air-tight container until ready to serve.

Note: Tamaulipas is a city in Mexico where this sauce originated.

SALSA DE MOLE

- 2 large white onions
- 6 cloves of peeled garlic
- 1 cup of pepitas
- 1 cup of shelled unsalted peanuts
- 4 guajillo chili or ancho chili (dried)
- ½ cup sesame seeds
- 4 large ripe tomatoes
- 500g dark unsweetened chocolate
- ¾ cup raisins
- crushed tortillas (plain)
- chicken or vegetable stock

In a large pot, heat the onion, garlic, pepitas, peanuts, chili, with oil for 35–40 minutes until color is dark and has a roasted aroma.

Add the tomatoes and continue to cook until all water had been cooked away.

Add chicken or vegetable stock until just covered, approximately 4 cups. Add sesame seeds, raisins, and crushed tortillas.

Cook for 2 hours on low heat, then cool, and pure in a blender. Blend until smooth, then pass through a sieve. The smoother your mole is the better it will taste.

In a stainless steel bowl add the chocolate, and place over a large pot, with approximately 10 cm (4 in) of water in it. The bowl should sit on top of the pot. Heat the water and the steam will melt the chocolate. When all is melted, pour into the mole until completely combined. Store in airtight container fridge. It will keep for approximately 1 month.

BASICS & SAUCES

SALSA PICO DE GALLO

- 6 ripe red tomatoes, diced
- 1 large white onion, diced
- 1 jalepeno (or serrano) deseeded, finely diced
- 1 bunch coriander (cilantro), washed and finely chopped
- 50 ml (1½ fl oz) fresh lime juice
- 1 tablespoon seasalt

Add all ingredients together and mix well. Store in the fridge in an air-tight container. Good for 3–5 days.

Note: Pico de gallo literally means 'beak of rooster'. It is also called salsa fresca.

BASICS & SAUCES

PICKLED CABBAGE

- 1 whole small red cabbage, julliened
- 2 large red onions cut, julliened
- 2 cups white vinegar
- 1 cup white sugar
- ½ cup salt

Place all of the ingredients into a mixing bowl and mix them thoroughly. Can be stored in an air-tight container for up to 1 week.

RECIPE INDEX

BEEF TACOS
TROPICAL TACOS   23
TACOS DE ALAMBRE   24
FAJITA TACOS   26
TINGA BEEF TACOS   27
ARRACHERA TACO   29
RIB EYE TACO WITH POTATOES AND PARSLEY   30
GUAJILLO BEEF TACOS   34
GRILLED FILLET STEAK TACOS   35
SIRLOIN ORANGE TACOS   37
BEEF TACOS WITH RED SAUCE   38

LAMB TACOS
LAMB AND BEER TACOS   43
LEG OF LAMB WITH APPLE TACOS   44
LAMB FILLET TACOS WITH SALSA MORITA   46
MARINATED LAMB TACO   47
LEMON LAMB TACOS   48
LAMB TACOS WITH COCONUT   51
LAMB NECK TACOS WITH MOLE   53
LAMB LOIN WITH PILONCILLO AND CHILI TACOS   55

PORK TACOS
PORK TACOS EN SALSA VERDE   59
PORK CARNITAS – MICHOACAN STYLE   60
SMOKED PORK CHOP TACOS   61
POBLANA TINGA TACOS   62
PORK AND PEANUT TACOS   65
PORK RIB TACOS WITH CHEESE   68
PORK APPLE TENDERLOIN TACOS   69
TACOS AL PASTOR   71
COCHINITA PIBIL TACOS   72

CHICKEN TACOS
CHICKEN ALAMBRE TACOS   76
CHICKEN SALPICON TACOS   79
CHICKEN POBLANO CHILI AND CORN TACOS   80
GRILLED CHICKEN TACOS   81
MULATO CHICKEN TACOS   84
CRUMBED CHICKEN TACOS   87
CHICKEN ONION JALAPEÑO TACOS   88
CHICKEN AND APPLE TACOS   93
CHICKEN TINGA TACOS   94

SEAFOOD TACOS
SHRIMP TACOS   99
FRIED FISH TACOS   100
SHRIMP COCONUT TACOS   103
CRAB TACOS   104
FISH WITH ORANGE TACOS   107
DIABLA SHIMP WITH CHEESE TACOS   108
MEXICAN OCTOPUS TACOS   111

VEGETARIAN TACOS
MUSHROOMS, ZUCCHINI AND SPINACH TACOS   114
BEAN AND SPINACH TACOS   116
PICO DE GALLO AND AVOCADO TACOS   119
GRILLED NOPALES TACOS   122
MUSHROOMS WITH GUAJILLO SAUCE TACOS   123
RAJAS POBLANAS WITH SOUR CREAM TACOS   126
PEPPERS WITH CHEESE TACOS   129

BASICS & SAUCES
HOMEMADE TORTILLAS   133
GUACAMOLE   134
CHILLED ONIONS   136
ROASTED TOMATOES   137
SOUR TOMATOES   137
SALSA ROJA   139
SALSA VERDE   142
SALSA HABANERO   145
SALSA TAMAULIPAS   146
SALSA DE MOLE   149
SALSA PICO DE GALLO   150
PICKLED CABBAGE   151

ACKNOWLEDGEMENTS

Los adoro.

To my brother, Jorge Antonio, for being a great inspiration and always being next to me. To my grandparents, who are one of the biggest role models and treasures in my life, with more than 50 years of marriage, and for sharing the love for cooking, family and for always being there.

To all my friends from Mexico City, Melbourne and Sydney Family it is a pleasure sharing this journey with you. To my mentor and big brother Carlito, grazie bello, and to all La Familia Amare, thank you from the bottom of my heart for amazing memories across these years.

I have been lucky enough to be able to follow my dream, to showcase a bit of my Mexico and culture in the other side of the world. Certainly there have been lessons along the way and I hope this is the beginning of another great stepping-stone in this journey we called life.

Thanks to chef Marco Antonio Méndez for his collaboration across the ocean. As the director of one of most respected cooking schools in Mexico, he has reviewed the recipes in this book making sure they are current with cooking trends in Mexico. Restaurants and chefs around the world are turning to the Mexican cuisine for inspiration. So, we hope you enjoy this journey through Mexico, our culture, our life.

MIKE ROUSSEAU

COOKING AND PLATING

Mike Rousseau is a Canadian born chef who has been travelling the world experimenting and learning new cuisines throughout his career. His culinary background stems from classic French bistro, but later gravitated to the simple, yet flavor filled tastes of the land south of his hometown of Vancouver, Mexico.

Travelling extensively throughout regional Mexico, he was intoduced to the traditional flavors, and history, and immediately fell in love with the food, culture, and eventually his wife Andrea Celeste, from Manzanillo. He currently has a hot sauce company called Diablo Sunrise which distibutes worldwide.

www.facebook.com/diablosunriseco

www.diablosunriseco@gmail.com

First published in 2017 by New Holland Publishers
London • Sydney • Auckland

The Chandlery, 50 Westminster Bridge Road, London SE1 7QY, United Kingdom
1/66 Gibbes Street, Chatswood, NSW 2067, Australia
5/39 Woodside Ave, Northcote, Auckland 0627, New Zealand

newhollandpublishers.com

Copyright © 2017 New Holland Publishers
Copyright © 2017 in text: Ricardo Amare del Castillo
Copyright © 2017 in images: New Holland Publishers

All rights reserved. No part of this publication may be reproduced, stored in a retrieval system or transmitted, in any form or by any means, electronic, mechanical, photocopying, recording or otherwise, without the prior written permission of the publishers and copyright holders.

A record of this book is held at the British Library and the National Library of Australia.

ISBN 9781742579764

Group Managing Director: Fiona Schultz
Publisher: Monique Butterworth
Project Editor: Susie Stevens
Proofreader: Kaitlyn Smith
Designer: Catherine Meachen
Photographer: Rebecca Elliott
Stylist: Tom Miles
Production Director: James Mills-Hicks
Printer: Hang Tai Printing Company Limited

10 9 8 7 6 5 4 3 2 1

Keep up with New Holland Publishers on Facebook
facebook.com/NewHollandPublishers